A Guide for Using

The Boxcar Children: Surprise Island

in the Classroom

Based on the novel written by Gertrude Chandler Warner

This guide written by **Donna Lee Long**

Teacher Created Materials, Inc.
6421 Industry Way
Westminster, CA 92683
www.teachercreated.com
©2000 Teacher Created Materials
Reprinted, 2003
Made in U.S.A.
ISBN 1-57690-338-9

Contributing Editor
Barbara Wally, M.S.

Illustrated by
Bruce Hedges

Cover Art by
Wendy Chang

Table of Contents

- Quiz Time
- Hands-On Project—*Mapping the Adventure*
- Cooperative Learning Activity—*Ready, Set, Go*
- Curriculum Connection—*How Many?*
- Into Your Life—*Reading Response Journals*

- Quiz Time
- Hands-on Project—*Drying Flowers*
- Cooperative Learning Activity—*Create a Class Museum*
- Curriculum Connection—*Cooking with Jessie*
- Into Your Life—*Nature Notes*

- Quiz Time
- Hands-on Project—*Painted Birds*
- Cooperative Learning Activity—*How Does Your Garden Grow?*
- Curriculum Connection—*Audubon's Art*
- Into Your Life—*Backyard Sanctuary*

- Quiz Time
- Hands-on Project—*Bird Banquet*
- Cooperative Learning Activity—*Can You Dig It?*
- Curriculum Connection—*On the Half Shell*
- Into Your Life—*An Island Cookbook*

- Quiz Time
- Hands-on Project—*Museum Brochures*
- Curriculum Connection—*How Mysterious*
- Cooperative Learning Activity—*Time Capsule*
- Into Your Life—*Meet the Aldens*

- Any Questions?
- Book Report Ideas

Introduction

A good book can touch our lives like a good friend. Within its pages are words and characters that can inspire us to achieve our highest ideals. We can turn to it for companionship, recreation, comfort, and guidance. It can also give us a cherished story to hold in our hearts forever.

In Literature Units great care has been taken to select books that are sure to become good friends. Teachers who use this literature unit will find the following features to supplement their own valuable ideas.

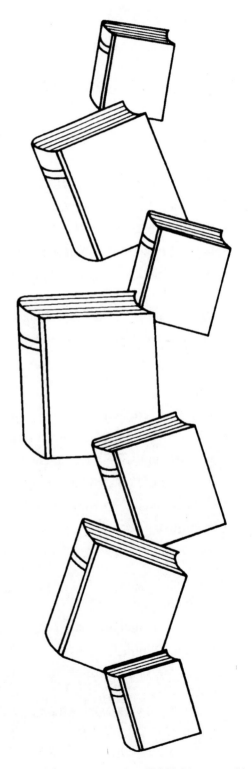

- sample lesson plans

- pre-reading activities

- a biographical sketch and picture of the author

- a book summary

- vocabulary lists and suggested vocabulary activities

- chapters grouped for study, with each section including:

  —a quiz

  —a hands-on project

  —a cooperative learning activity

  —a cross-curricular connection

  —an extension into the reader's life

- post-reading activities

- generic activities for any boxcar mystery

- two options for unit tests

- bibliography of related reading

- answer key

We are confident this unit will be a valuable addition to your lesson planning. Through the use of these ideas, we hope that your students will increase their circle of book "friends."

Sample Lesson Plans

Each of the lessons below may take from one to several days to complete.

Lesson 1
- Complete activity 1 on page 5.
- Read About the Author with the students (page 6).
- Do some or all of the pre-reading activities (page 5).
- Introduce the vocabulary list for Section 1 (page 8).

Lesson 2
- Read chapters 1–3.
- Select a vocabulary activity (page 9).
- Complete the math activity (page 13).
- Create a map of the island (page 11).
- Plan an expedition to an island (page 12).
- Begin Reading Response Journals (page 14).
- Administer Section 1 quiz (page 10).
- Introduce vocabulary for Section 2 (page 8).

Lesson 3
- Read chapters 4–6.
- Select a vocabulary activity (page 9).
- Establish a classroom museum (page 17).
- Practice adjusting a recipe (page 18).
- Begin nature observations (page 19).
- Collect and dry flowers (page 16).
- Administer Section 2 quiz (page 15).
- Introduce Section 3 vocabulary (page 8).

Lesson 4
- Read chapters 7–9.
- Select a vocabulary activity (page 9).
- Design a wildlife sanctuary (page 24).
- Read about painter John James Audubon (page 23).
- Create painted birds for the class museum (page 21).

- Plan a vegetable garden (page 22).
- Administer Section 3 quiz (page 20).
- Introduce Section 4 vocabulary (page 8).

Lesson 5
- Read chapters 10–12.
- Select a vocabulary activity (page 9).
- Prepare a banquet for birds (page 26).
- Complete the archaeology activity (page 27).
- Explore clam expressions (page 28).
- Create a cookbook of island recipes (page 29).
- Administer Section 4 quiz (page 25).
- Introduce Section 5 vocabulary (page 8).

Lesson 6
- Read chapters 13–15.
- Select a vocabulary activity (page 9).
- Prepare museum brochures (page 31).
- Write a mystery (page 32).
- Create a time capsule (page 33).
- Compare yourself to the Aldens (page 34).
- Administer Section 5 quiz (page 30).

Lesson 7
- Review the story using one or more of the activities on pages 37–42.
- Discuss any questions your students may have (page 35).
- Assign research projects (page 35) and/or book reports (page 36).
- Plan and conduct the culminating activity (page 43).
- Administer the unit test of your choice for evaluation (pages 44 and 45).

Before the Book

Before you begin reading *Surprise Island* with your students, do some pre-reading activities to stimulate interest and enhance comprehension. Here are some activities that may work for your students. You may want to add others.

1. Explain who the Boxcar Children are by providing a short summary of the first book of the series, *The Boxcar Children*. If time allows, *The Boxcar Children* may be read aloud by the teacher before beginning the *Surprise Island* study. Reading two or three chapters a day would complete the book in a week.

2. Show the children the cover of *Surprise Island*. Read the title and ask them to predict what the story might be about.

3. Discuss surprises by asking questions like the following:

    • Do you like surprises?
    • Can they be good or bad?
    • What are some surprises you have had?
    • What surprises do you think we might read about in the story?

4. Discuss what types of things one would expect to see on an island. What things would you need to take along if you were going to live on an island?

5. Discuss answers to the following questions or use them as topics for writing assignments or journal writing.

Are you interested in—	Would you like to—
• mystery stories?	• live on an island?
• stories about nature?	• be on your own?
• stories about families?	• do your own cooking?
• stories about adventure?	• travel by boat?
	• explore nature?
	• discover things from past civilizations?
	• live the entire summer without TV, radio, or CD/tape player?

About the Author

Gertrude Chandler Warner was born in 1890 in Putnam, Connecticut. As a child she lived near a train station. Warner was intrigued by the little stove and coffeepot she glimpsed inside a caboose and wondered what it might be like to live in a train car. Warner was also an avid reader and writer of stories about her family.

Although ill health kept her from graduating from high school, Warner was asked to teach first grade during a World War I teacher shortage, a position she held for 30 years. Warner never married. Instead, she devoted her life to her students, to her tireless work with the Red Cross, and to her music. She was an accomplished cellist and played the organ for her church.

As a teacher, Warner found that it was difficult to find books for her students that were both interesting and easy to read. She decided to solve this problem by writing books herself. She carefully chose young characters with whom her students could relate, placed them in a variety of unique and adventuresome situations, and gave them real-life problems to solve. She also encouraged resourcefulness and thinking in her students by having the characters solve these problems on their own with as little adult help as possible. The books were written in simple language so that her students might enjoy the story rather than stumble through words they did not understand.

As an adult, she was often ill and would write to pass the time while she was recuperating. Her first book, *The Boxcar Children*, was written while recovering from an illness. By having the characters set up housekeeping in an abandoned railroad car, Warner brought her childhood vision to life. Her efforts were well received by children, and she continued writing new adventures for the Alden children. Warner was 86 when she wrote the last of the 19 books in the original series. In addition to *The Boxcar Children* books, Warner wrote four books for adults and 12 nonfiction books for children.

Gertrude Chandler Warner died in 1979, but *The Boxcar Children Mysteries* continue to bring joy and a love of reading to new generations of children.

Surprise Island

by Gertrude Chandler Warner

(Albert Whitman, 1989)

(Available in Canada from General Publishing; in U.K. from Bakerd Taylor International; in AUS from Stafford International)

Summary

The Alden children are delighted when their grandfather arranges for them to spend the summer by themselves on an island. They plan a summer of swimming and nature exploration. A mysterious handyman and the discovery of ancient Indian relics add much to the excitement. The children use their knowledge and resourcefulness to discover the truth behind a series of curious events.

The Boxcar Children Mystery Series

Introduced in 1942, *The Boxcar Children* books continue to be favorites with young readers. At first, many librarians felt that the children were having too much fun without adult supervision. Children liked the book for that very reason. The exciting adventures of the Alden children are told in easy-to-read chapters. Children as young as second grade can read them on their own, while the exciting stories hold the attention of older students.

In the first book, *The Boxcar Children*, the four Alden children—Henry, Jessie, Violet, and Benny—are orphans. They are afraid of living with the grandfather they have never met and are running away. They soon find an abandoned boxcar, which they turn into a home with dishes and household items they find in a nearby dump. Henry finds work doing odd jobs for kind Dr. Moore, who quickly discovers the children's identity. He sees that they are able to earn plenty of money for food and necessities but does not reveal their whereabouts. When Violet becomes ill, the children are forced to move into Dr. Moore's home where they meet kind "Mr. Henry," who is ultimately revealed to be their grandfather. All ends happily when grandfather has the boxcar moved to the garden of his elegant home, where the children will live with him, so that the children may visit it whenever they wish.

In the many subsequent books, Henry, Jessie, Violet, and Benny are placed in a variety of unique and exotic places and circumstances. In each book they solve one mystery after another using their common sense and skills of deduction. Miss Warner wrote the first 19 books of the series. Authors who remain true to the spirit of the original books have written additional books. The characters are depicted as ever kind, independent, and resourceful—qualities that endear *The Boxcar Children* to succeeding generations of children.

Vocabulary Lists

The vocabulary lists on this page correspond to each sectional grouping of chapters. Ideas for vocabulary activities can be found on page 9 of this book.

Section 1: *Chapter 1–3*

surprise	shell	rather
explore	housekeeping	dock
ocean	twinkle	handy
mainland	hut	stranger
appeared	delicious	spring
delighted	groceries	weed
lobster	cupboard	enough
island	clever	
captain	stalls	

Section 2: *Chapter 4–6*

seaweed	beach	kettle
interesting	careful	perfect
clamming	sweater	settled
queer	collection	cleaning
stream	dozen	museum
feathery	raft	smoothed
worried	guest	beautiful

Section 3: *Chapter 7–9*

arrowhead	skeleton	tide
camera	fisherman	holes
rocky	company	howl
wampum	violin	broken
fishhook	scared	selfish
bait	whole	Indian
crossly	doorway	pictures
suddenly	dressing	twin
arrow	remember	
quahogs	practice	

Section 4: *Chapter 10–12*

certainly	bottle	empty
invite	important	blankets
waving	pointed	package
rolling pin	hungry	lucky
awfully	rowboat	crust
chowder	spite	trouble
wonderful	frightened	

Section 5: *Chapter 13–15*

lesson	frosting	promised
exactly	float	notice
candles	telephone	basket
tablecloth	cousin	weekends
understands	scrambled	veins
birthday	uncle	different
lonesome	claws	

8

Vocabulary Activities

❏ **Vocabulary Baseball**

Divide your class into two teams and set up a baseball diamond with a soft ball that can be thrown in the classroom. The batter either spells a vocabulary word or gives the definition of the vocabulary word given to them by the pitcher. If the batter answers correctly, the pitcher throws the ball. The batter uses his or her hand as a bat. Switch teams when there are three outs.

❏ **Vocabulary Bee**

Follow the pattern of a traditional spelling bee to conduct a Vocabulary Bee. Challenge the students to give the correct definition of the word as well as the correct spelling. Have students find the root word for each vocabulary word. They may then create new words by adding prefixes or suffixes to the root word. Have a contest to see who can discover the most new words.

❏ **Quick Thinking**

Give each student a card with one of the vocabulary words on it. Allow a few minutes of "thinking time" for him or her to make up a sentence using that vocabulary word correctly. If you are teaching a lesson on plot sequence, have the students concentrate on using their words to retell the narrative. As an enrichment activity, ask the students to use their sentences as the topic sentence for an original story.

❏ **Puzzles**

Provide large-squared graph paper and allow your students to create their own word search or crossword puzzles using the vocabulary words. These can then be photocopied and used to provide their classmates practice in identifying vocabulary words.

As a group activity, have students work together to create an illustrated dictionary of the vocabulary words. Use the vocabulary words for dictionary practice. Ask students to do one or more of the following:

- Find the words in the dictionary.
- Identify the part(s) of speech for each.

- Divide the words into syllables.
- Find words with more than one definition. (Which word has the most definitions?)

❏ **Matching Game**

Write the vocabulary words on index cards and tape them onto the chalkboard. Write the definitions of these vocabulary words on index cards and place these in a pile on a table. Divide your class into teams of four or five. Students take turns drawing a card with a definition. They then have 30 seconds to match the definition with the vocabulary word. If they match it correctly, they get a point. If they do not, the definition goes to the bottom of the pile and the next team takes a turn.

❏ **Quiz Show**

Have students illustrate the vocabulary words on one side of a sheet of paper. The word is written on the back. These can be used as a "quiz show" for a whole-class activity, with one student acting as moderator, or they can be placed on a bulletin board or hallway display with the words added at the bottom. As a variation, students may do impromptu drawings on the chalkboard, challenging classmates to guess the word.

Quiz Time

1. On the back of this paper, list three events that happened in the first three chapters of *Surprise Island*.

2. What is the children's surprise?

   _____

3. Do you think the Alden children have lived alone before? Why or why not?

   _____

   _____

4. What things do the children pack to take to the island?

   _____

   _____

5. What does Benny think is the most important thing to take along?

   _____

6. Who might Joe, the handyman, be and why is he being so mysterious?

   _____

   _____

7. How do the children get supplies?

   _____

   _____

8. What is Benny's job each day?

   _____

   _____

9. Do you think Henry, Jessie, Violet, and Benny are good problem solvers? Why?

   _____

   _____

   _____

10. Tell what Jessie meant when she said, "Everything seems better when we have to work to get it." How do you feel about what Jessie said? Write your answer on the back of this paper.

   _____

   _____

Mapping the Adventure

One of the adventures facing the Alden children is exploring the island that will be their home for the summer. As you read about their adventures, locate the physical features of the island and the places the children visit on the island map below. Some are listed in the box below. Add any others you may find in your reading. Make different shapes for each place, using crayons, markers, or colored pencils. Create a key or legend that explains what each shape represents. You may use words or pictures for the legend.

Extension: Use clay or papier-mâché to create a model of the island. Add features using sticks, small pebbles, sand, etc.

Key / Legend

- barn
- Captain Daniel's hut
- yellow house
- apple trees
- garden
- dock
- clam beach
- swimming beach
- Indian Point
- shell pie
- cave
- treasure chest

Ready, Set, Go

You and your friends have been invited to spend a school vacation on a private island, much like the Alden children. The island has a barn for shelter, and there is a working stove. Everything else must be bought from the mainland. Work as a group to make a list of things you will need for your stay on the island. Remember, you must be able to carry the items in a small motorboat.

Use the categories below to organize your list.

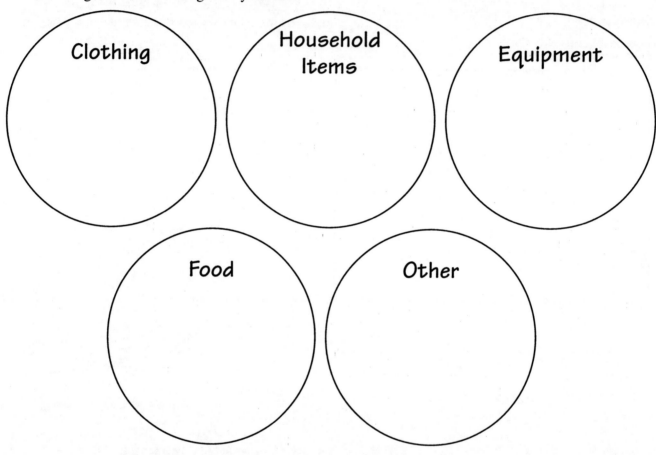

Now decide what things need to be done and who will do each chore.

Name	Chore

How Many?

Use your multiplication facts to solve the following math mysteries. Write the answers for each on the lines.

1. Henry, Jessie, Violet, and Benny each ate three bowls of clam chowder. How many bowls of chowder were eaten all together? _____

2. Joe brought books about butterflies, fish, flowers, and seashells. He brought two books about each. How many books did he bring? _____

3. In the garden, there were three rows each of peas and onions. How many rows were there? _____

4. Henry, Jessie, Violet, Benny, and Watch each ate three slices of bread with their milk for supper. How many slices of bread were eaten? _____

5. Jessie bought six each of the spoons, cups, bowls, and plates for the island. How many items did Jessie buy? _____

6. Violet made a seaweed collection. She put two kinds of seaweed on each sheet of paper. She used six sheets of papers. How many kinds of seaweed were in Violet's collection? _____

7. The Aldens went exploring. Henry, Jessie, Violet, and Benny each put five shells into the kettle. How many shells were in the kettle? _____

8. Jessie and Violet each made seven paper birds for the museum. How many birds did they make? _____

9. Benny helped Henry put shells into the boxes for the museum. They had three boxes. If they put six shells in each box, how many shells were there? _____

10. Benny said that Joe gets two newspapers every day. How many newspapers does Joe get in a week? _____

Reading Response Journals

One excellent way to ensure that reading of literature becomes a personal experience for each student is to include the use of reading response journals in your plans. In these journals, students can be encouraged to respond to the story in a number of ways. Here are a few ideas.

❑ Tell students that the purpose of the journal is to record their thoughts, ideas, observations, and questions as they read.

❑ Provide students with, or ask them to suggest, topics from the story that would stimulate writing. Specific examples include the following:

- situations provoking strong emotions, such as anger, fear, or great admiration.

- situations which are ambiguous, unclear, or cause puzzlement and wonder.

- conditions, occupations, or subjects about which they like to know more about, such as life at sea, veterinary work, crafts, electronics, flying, space, or anything else personally engaging.

❑ After reading each chapter, students can write one or more new things they learned in the chapter.

❑ Have students use a double-entry journal by writing one short quote that interests them from each chapter on the left side of their paper. On the right side, they should express their own ideas about the quote.

❑ Ask students to draw their responses to certain events or characters in the story, using blank pages in their journals.

❑ Tell students that they may use their journals to record "diary-type" responses that they may want to enter.

❑ Give students quotes from the novel and ask them to write their own responses. Make sure to do this before you go over the quotations in class. In groups they could list the different ways each responded to the same quote.

❑ Allow students time to write in their journals daily.

❑ The teacher will read personal reflections, but no corrections or letter grades will be assigned. Credit is given for effort, and all students who sincerely try will be awarded credit. If a grade is desired for this type of entry, grade according to the number of journal entries completed. For example, if five journal assignments were made and the student conscientiously completes all five, then he or she receives an "A."

❑ Nonjudgmental teacher responses should be made to let the students know you enjoy their journals. Here are some types of responses that will please your journal writers and encourage them to write more.

- *"You have really found what's important in the story!"*

- *"You write so clearly, I almost feel as if I am there."*

- *"If you feel comfortable, I'd like you to share this with the class. I think they'll enjoy it as much as I have."*

Quiz Time

1. On the back of this paper, list three events that happened in chapters 4–6.

2. How does Henry know where the clams are?

   _____

   _____

3. Who helps dig up the clams?

   _____

   _____

4. Why doesn't Benny want to go swimming? How does Joe get him to go into the water?

   _____

   _____

5. Why does Henry think that Joe is a strange handyman?

   _____

   _____

6. What is Henry's great idea? Do the other children like his idea?

   _____

   _____

7. Do you think Joe knows much about books and libraries? Why or why not?

   _____

   _____

   _____

8. How does Benny know that Joe would have some old newspapers?

   _____

   _____

9. What happens when it begins to rain during the night?

   _____

   _____

   _____

10. When Henry asks Joe, "How did you ever learn all this?" Joe said, "Oh, I just picked it up." What did he mean by that?

    _____

    _____

Drying Flowers

Violet and Jessie decided to preserve flowers for their museum. They did it by placing the flowers between sheets of newspaper. They put a board over the newspapers and added a weight.

Materials

• fresh flowers   • newspapers   • heavy hardcover books   • index cards   • poster board

Directions

Select the flowers, leaves, or grasses that you will use for the project. Look for different colors and shapes. You can try pressing any kind of flowers or plants, but delicate flowers with a single layer of petals work best. Some suggestions are wood violets, Queen Anne's Lace, Baby-Blue-Eyes, Lupine (the leaves are great to press too), Lobelia, Phlox, Verbena, Pansies, Viola, Azalea, soft foliage of ferns, and Lace-leaf Dusty Miller. (Flowers like roses, lilies, and tulips with a high water content or bulky form will take longer to dry and may develop mold. For these flowers, press individual petals or carefully cut the flower in half.)

Try to find the best quality flowers and petals. Pick the flowers on a dry day, preferably in the morning. Place two pieces of newspaper on the table or counter. Lay the flowers one by one on the newspaper. Make sure that they are flat and do not touch each other. Place two more pieces of newspaper over the top of the flowers. Carefully set a large, heavy book on top of the newspaper.

Place more heavy books on top of the book with the flowers. The purpose is to keep out the air and light so the flowers dry flat and smooth. Check the flowers for dryness after one week. If they are not quite dry, simply set the books on top again and check in a few more days.

While you are waiting for the flowers to dry, find as much information as you can about the flowers. Record your findings on an index card. When the flowers are dry, use white glue to mount them on a piece of poster board. Add the index cards with the details to the display.

Extensions

If you have duplicate flowers or would like to find other uses for your pressed flowers, try one of these ideas.

❏ **Make Cards**

Fold a piece of cardstock into the size card you would like to make. Arrange a few of your dried pressed flowers on the front of the card. Cut a piece of sticky-back plastic large enough to cover the front of your card (or slightly smaller). Very carefully lay the clear sticky plastic over the flowers. This is tricky as the flowers want to jump up onto the plastic. Gently rub to seal the plastic to the card. You may want to draw a border on the card before putting the flowers on for a little extra artistry.

❏ **Keep a Flower Album**

You can create an album of the flowers and herbs you find growing in your area. Use a photo album that has peel-back pages. Place the flowers in the photo album.

❏ **Frame Your Flowers**

Arrange the dried flowers on a piece of heavy paper and insert them in a small picture frame.

Create a Class Museum

The children decided to collect items from their island and create a museum in the barn. Grandfather donated money to build a large museum for the city. You can create your own museum, right in your own classroom!

A museum is a building, place, or institution devoted to collecting, preserving, studying, and interpreting objects that have scientific, historical, or artistic value. The objects chosen must be suitable for exhibition, for study purposes, or both. Each item must be documented with well-organized information accompanying the display.

Decide as a class what kinds of items you will include in your museum. Brainstorm and record suggestions of items from nature for your museum. Assign members of the class to collect specimens. You may want to ask parents and friends if they have collections of shells, butterflies, etc., that they would loan to the class for exhibition.

Work with your teacher to create a space for your displays. It may be as simple as an empty bookcase, a display in the school library, or a table or ledge with a banner or sign above it, such as "Mrs. Smith's Third-Grade Museum."

Prepare identification cards for each item in the display. If items are borrowed, include the name of the owner on the card.

When you have finished your museum, invite other classes and/or parents to view your collections. Assign members of the class to act as interpreters, explaining the various displays. Caution visitors that the displays are to be seen only and that no touching is allowed.

Name: _____

Found: _____

_____

_____

Interesting Facts: _____

_____

_____

_____

Contributed by: _____

_____

_____

Cooking with Jessie

Jessie likes to cook for her family and friends. Sometimes when extra guests are staying for dinner, Jessie needs to make more than one recipe of something in order to have enough for everyone.

Choose a favorite recipe that does not require too many ingredients or elaborate preparation. In the space provided, write the ingredients needed to prepare one recipe. Imagine that you have to double or triple the recipe in order to serve more people. Calculate to find the ingredient amounts for two and three recipes and write the answers in the correct columns. Write directions for preparing the food. Use the back of this paper if needed. If possible, have a group of friends use this form to prepare their favorite recipes and make a cookbook titled, "Cooking for the Crowd," or "Crowd-Pleaser Recipes."

Recipe for _____

Ingredients

One Recipe   **Two Recipes**   **Three Recipes**

Directions

_____

_____

_____

_____

_____

_____

_____

Nature Notes

Prepare a diary to keep a record of interesting things that you observe. This will serve as a reference for items in your museum and for your writing.

Make copies of the form below. Bind them in a booklet, using construction paper or other heavy paper as a cover. If you wish, decorate the cover with a nature design. Describe and/or draw the plants, birds, butterflies, insects, etc., that you observe. Be as specific as possible in your description. Include information about where you see each item. If you do not know the name of the plant or creature, use the description to help you find it in a reference book.

Day _____   Date_____

Category_____

Common Name _____   Drawing

Scientific Name _____

Where Seen_____

Description_____

_____

_____

_____

_____

_____

_____

Quiz Time

1. On the back of this paper, list three events that happened in chapters 7–9.

2. Who had lived in the cave the children found?

   _____

   _____

3. What dangerous thing happened at the cave?

   _____

   _____

4. Tell what you think of Joe now? Why do you think he is so excited about the cave and the shell pile?

   _____

   _____

   _____

5. How does Joe know that someone once lived on the island?

   _____

   _____

6. Why does Joe ask Benny, Watch, and Violet to sit beside the shell pile while he takes a picture?

   _____

   _____

7. How does Joe know the bone Benny finds is not a horse bone?

   _____

   _____

8. Why must the children keep the digging site a secret?

   _____

   _____

9. What does Henry name the digging place?

   _____

   _____

10. Why does Violet cry?

   _____

   _____

   _____

Painted Birds

The Alden children made painted birds to display in their museum. You can make your own painted birds. Begin by observing and listing the birds in your local area. Choose one or more from the list and research basic facts about it. What is its size and color? What does it eat? Does it have any interesting characteristics? Does it remain in your area all year or does it migrate?

Materials

- heavy paper or brown paper bags
- paintbrushes
- clay
- pencils

- poster paints
- twigs or other sticks
- glue or tape
- cotton balls or polyester stuffing (optional)

Directions

1. Make copies of the generic bird pattern below on cardstock and cut them out. Enlarge the pattern to make it life-size. You may wish to make several different sizes, depending on the birds chosen by the students.

2. Ask the children to trace around the pattern on the heavy brown paper. Tell them to add other details and make any changes that might be needed in the shape of the beak, wings, or heads.

3. Paint the birds and allow them to dry.

4. Cut out the birds and use tape to attach each bird to a twig. Stick the twigs into small balls of clay so that they stand up.

5. To create three-dimensional birds, have the children make two copies of their birds. Glue or staple the edges of the two birds together, leaving a small opening. Stuff lightly with cotton or batting and close the opening.

Other items like nests made of leaves and sticks, paper bird eggs, or paper flowers may be added to the arrangement, if desired and if the supplies are available. These make a nice addition to the classroom museum.

How Does Your Garden Grow?

The Alden children are happy to find a garden has been planted for them on the island. Many of their meals feature fresh vegetables from their garden. Nutritionists tell us that people should eat three to five servings of fruits and vegetables each day.

Work in small groups to plan a garden that will provide fresh vegetables for the group throughout the summer. Notice that different vegetables take different amounts of time to grow. Try to select crops that will be ready at different times.

Choose your favorite vegetables from the chart. If your favorite is not listed, research it and add it to the chart.

Decide how much of each you should plant to feed all the members of your group. Use the information about plant spacing to determine how large the garden should be.

Draw your garden on the back of this paper. If you prefer, you may cut pictures of the plants from magazines and catalogs and paste them to the plot.

Make a plan for tending the garden.

What is the earliest planting date for your area? When will the first vegetables be ready to eat?

Garden Vegetables			
Plants	Spacing	Amount per Person	Time to Grow
Beans	plants 4" (10 cm) apart rows 3–4 feet (about 1 m) apart	5 feet (1.5 m)	50–60 days
Carrots	plants 2" (5 cm) apart rows 2 feet (about .6 m) apart	4–5 feet (about 1.4 m)	50 days
Onions	plants 4" (10 cm) apart rows 12" (about 30 cm) apart	4–5 feet (about 1.4 m)	50–60 days
Peas	plants 1" (2.5 cm) apart rows 3 feet (about 1 m) apart	10 feet (3 m)	55–78 days

Extensions

- Bring your garden plan to life by planting a class garden. If room is not available for an outdoor garden, use containers in the classroom.

- Keep a record of what you eat for one week. How many servings of fruits and vegetables did you eat each day?

Audubon's Art

John James Audubon was an American artist best known for his realistic portrayals of American birds and wildlife. Fascinated by the abundant wildlife of America, Audubon proved in 1809 that migrating birds returned to the same location. His method was simple. He attached fine pieces of thread to the legs of several birds. The following year he observed that his marked birds had returned.

In 1838 he published his masterpiece, *The Birds of America*. The book consists of 435 hand-colored folio plates depicting 1,065 species of birds in life size. A second book by Audubon and Scottish naturalist William MacGillivray, *The Ornithological Biography*, described the characteristics and habits of the birds he had painted. Later, the books were combined in a seven-volume set called *The Birds of America*. Few of the original books with the hand-colored drawings remain, but Audubon's work has been preserved and is often reproduced.

The National Audubon Society, named for John James Audubon, is a private organization whose purpose is to conserve and restore ecosystems. Its work focuses on the importance of birds and other wildlife for the benefit of humanity and Earth's biological diversity. The Audubon Society conducts a variety of programs to educate the public about the need to conserve soil, water, plants, and wildlife and to encourage appreciation for the world around us.

Activities

1. Since Audubon painted his famous birds, several of them have become extinct, and others have become endangered species. Brainstorm a list of extinct and endangered birds. If you have access to the Internet, the following Web sites can provide a list:

   - *http://eelink.net/Endspp.old.bak/Endangered.html*

   - *http://endangered.fws.gov/endspp.html*

2. As a class, discuss what you can do to aid in protecting endangered species. What is the importance of Audubon's paintings and natural history museums in telling the story?

3. Select a bird that you have observed. Is it migratory? If so, research its range and use yarn or string to mark its migratory route on a classroom map.

Backyard Sanctuary

Because only a few people live on Surprise Island, there are many different kinds of birds, butterflies, and wildflowers for the Alden children to observe. In many places, people and buildings have disturbed the natural environment, making it difficult for wildlife to survive. Some communities have parks and areas set aside to preserve the natural habitat of native birds and animals. One name for these areas is *sanctuary*, which means a place of safety.

You can turn your backyard into a miniature sanctuary by providing several different kinds of plants and flowers to attract birds and butterflies.

Here are some suggestions for flowers and plants that are especially attractive to various birds and butterflies.

- Cosmos and sunflowers are good sources of pollen for butterflies and seeds for finches.

- Zinnias, a favorite of butterflies, are easy to grow.

- Strawberries provide food for birds, turtles, and people.

There are many more plants and flowers that butterflies, hummingbirds, and other birds like. Remember that many birds eat the insects that flowers attract, as well as seeds of the plants. Some other flowers to consider are listed below.

Amaranthus	Celosia	Portulaca
Asters	Coreopsis	Rudbeckia
Bachelor's Buttons	Echinacea	Scabiosa
Calendula	Millet	Thistles
Chrysanthemums	Phlox	Verbena

Herbs like dill, parsley, and fennel are food sources for the caterpillars that will become butterflies. You will see many butterflies if you provide a place for them to raise young right in your own yard.

Provide a dish of water or a bird bath. For an experiment, dust the area around the dish with flour and see the tracks of all the animals that visit your water dish.

Answer these questions.

1. What types of birds would you like to attract? _____

   _____

2. What flowers are in your yard now? What flowers will you add? _____

   _____

3. On the back of this paper, draw a picture of your sanctuary. Remember to show the birds and butterflies.

Quiz Time

1. On the back of this paper, list three events that happened in this section.

2. What does Grandfather think of the children? How can you tell?

   _____

   _____

3. Why does Jessie think Grandfather might not want to go upstairs?

   _____

   _____

4. What does Grandfather have to show the children?

   _____

   _____

5. Why do you think Joe does not want Grandfather to see him?

   _____

   _____

   _____

6. Who is the stranger who comes to dinner? Why is he on the island?

   _____

   _____

7. What makes Mr. Browning think that Joe is the person he is looking for?

   _____

   _____

8. Who finds the buried treasure?

   _____

   _____

9. How do Pat and Johnny get the rowboat?

   _____

   _____

10. What does Morris mean when he says, "Everybody ought to know how to swim."

   _____

   _____

Bird Banquet

One sure-fire way to attract birds so that you can watch them is to invite them to dinner. How many birds and what kinds of birds will use your feeder depends on the time of year and on what you serve. Birds may be attracted to fruit, seeds, insects, or nectar. Feeding stations are more popular when natural food sources are scarce. Use one of the ideas below to create a bird feeding station from materials you can find around the house or come up with your own design.

Bird Food Garlands

String popped corn, bits of fruit, and bread on loops of thread. Hang the loops over branches of trees.

Pie Plate Feeder

Attach an old pie tin to an old broom handle or dowel with a nail. Place the dowel or broom handle in the ground and serve a variety of seeds in the pie plate.

Pine Cone Feeders

Roll a large pine cone in thin, sugary icing and then in seeds. If you prefer, you can stuff bits of bread and fruit into the pine cone. Hang the completed feeder on a branch with string.

Corn on the Cob

Many birds like corn. Select a fresh ear of corn. Peel back the husk and remove the silk. Tie the corn to a branch with string.

Plastic Container Feeder

Cut a hole in the side of a well-washed, one-gallon plastic drink or milk container. Tie a string through the handle and hang it from a tree. Fill the bottom of the container with birdseed.

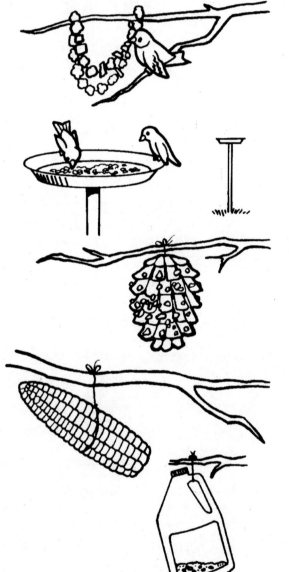

Suggestions

Try a variety of different foods from the list below to create your feed mix. Keep a record that shows which kinds of birds prefer which type of food.

- *Fruit:* apples, grapes, oranges, tomatoes, plums, peaches, raisins (soaked)
- *Fat (replaces insects):* suet, peanut butter*
- *Seeds and Nuts:* millet, cracked corn, unsalted sunflower seeds, unsalted nut meats

Be sure to provide a source of water.

Experts also advise including some fine sand or gravel or crushed egg shells in the mix to aid in the birds' digestion.

Note:

*Peanut butter will not harm birds, but it is difficult for them to swallow. Experts suggest mixing it with lard, cornmeal, or grit before feeding it to the birds.

Can You Dig It?

Archaeologists and anthropologists use artifacts and sites to help tell the stories of ancient peoples. By examining the artifacts, they try to understand the lives and beliefs of past civilizations. Sometimes the artifacts have been altered by the elements. At other times, the objects and their uses are unknown. It is important to record the exact location of each item in a particular dig site. Often scientists can draw conclusions about an object from other things that are around it.

Follow the directions below to conduct an archaeological expedition in the classroom.

Materials *(for each group)*

- cardboard carton
- spoons or garden trowels
- small paintbrushes
- beads
- pieces of broken pottery
- feathers

- sand
- a piece of coarse screen
- a collection of small household items like buttons
- tools
- costume jewelry
- poultry bones (boil to remove any flesh), etc.

Directions

1. Work in a small group, examine each object, and brainstorm all the possible uses for it.

2. Work together to write a story about a people who once used these objects. What were their likes, dislikes, and values? How did they live?

3. Bury the objects in sand in a carton. Remember to place related objects near each other and to place the groups of objects at different levels in the sand.

4. Exchange boxes and begin excavating. It is important to work slowly and methodically, using a small implement. Even very small fragments can help tell the story, so sand should be sifted through a screen as it is removed. When an artifact is found, treat it with respect and care. Use a brush to remove any debris from the artifact.

5. Record each artifact as it is found.

6. Once you have found all the objects and charted their locations, write your conclusions about the people who once used them. Compare your conclusions to the story written by the group that prepared the site.

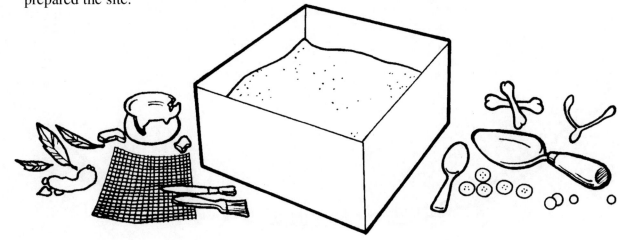

On the Half Shell

Joe tells the children some important facts about clams. Learn more about this interesting mollusk by completing the activities below. Write your responses on a separate sheet of paper.

1. Write the dictionary definition of clam.

2. Use context clues to explain the "clam" expressions below. What do they mean? How did clam come to be used in this way?

    a. He paid 25 *clams* for his radio.

    b. Before Benny could answer, Henry told him to *clam up*.

    c. When she played the violin, Violet was as happy as a *clam* at high tide.

    d. The children feasted on *clam* chowder.

    e. We were invited to a *clambake* on the beach.

    f. Jessie wore her new sweater and a pair of blue *clam diggers*.

Use the pattern below to make a booklet. Cut two "shells" from construction paper for the covers and several pages from lined paper. Staple them together at the top. Choose one of the following activities and write your answers in the clam book.

- Research one or more varieties of clams. Tell where it is found, how it is used, and any other interesting facts you find.

- Write a story about a clam or use one of the expressions above in telling a story.

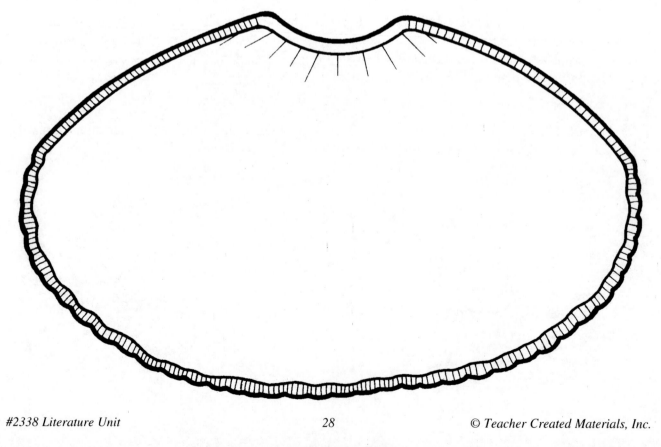

An Island Cookbook

As they explored the island, the Alden children gathered food for their meals. They also spent part of their time preparing the food they needed. As a class, make a list of the foods that the Aldens ate. Which foods were collected on the island and which ones came from the mainland? Add other foods that might be available to someone living on an island.

Choose one or more of the foods from the list. Find or create a recipe for the food you have chosen. Write your recipe on the card below. Be sure to include complete measurements, a list of any special equipment needed, and the steps for preparing your dish. Copy the completed recipes and bind them into a booklet to share with parents or display them on a bulletin board with a caption, such as "See What We Have Cooked Up" or "Look What's Cooking in Our Class."

Recipe for _____

_____

_____

_____

_____

_____

_____

_____

_____

_____

_____

_____

_____

_____

Extensions

- Prepare your recipe at home and bring samples to share with members of the class.

- Exchange recipes with a classmate and follow his or her directions exactly. Did the recipe produce the desired result?

Quiz Time

1. On the back of this paper, tell three events that happened in this section.

2. What did Benny want for his birthday? Why?

   _____

   _____

3. How do the Alden children feel about Joe being their cousin?

   _____

   _____

4. Tell why you think Joe has been hiding on the island.

   _____

   _____

5. Why was Benny allowed to be the one to call Grandfather?

   _____

   _____

6. Why did Mr. Browning suggest that Grandfather not see Joe suddenly?

   _____

   _____

7. What was the island named? Why was it called this?

   _____

   _____

8. Who knew all summer who Joe was, and why he was on the island?

   _____

   _____

9. What will happen to the things in the cave and near the shell pile?

   _____

   _____

10. Who is the children's real best friend?

   _____

   _____

Museum Brochures

How will you let people know about your new museum and its exhibits? One way is to prepare a brochure that provides basic information about your museum.

Materials

- paper
- pencil
- markers
- glue
- magazines

Directions

1. As a class look at a variety of brochures or pamphlets. Discuss the size and format, type of information included, pictures, and other features of the brochures. Make a list of the variations on the chalkboard.

2. Notice that the brochures describe the place being advertised, making it sound wonderful and interesting. In the space below, brainstorm a list of words that describe the museum and make it sound appealing.

Word List

---

3. Work in small groups to produce a brochure advertising the Alden children's museum or the class museum, as your teacher directs. The brochures should include several paragraphs of writing to describe the purpose of the museum and its importance, and to persuade the reader to visit the museum, and to give information on the hours, location, etc. Cut from magazines or draw pictures that illustrate the museum and its contents.

4. Display the finished brochures on a bulletin board. If desired, select one or more brochures to duplicate for use at the museum's grand opening celebration.

Extension

Use your brochure-making technique to create a booklet that explains one of the following and share it with visitors to your museum:

- museum terms and etiquette for younger students
- archaeological techniques
- John James Audubon's art

How Mysterious

Many people enjoy reading mystery books because they enjoy trying to solve the mystery as the story goes along. A good mystery author gives the reader clues, a little at a time, throughout the story. There should be enough hints to keep the story interesting and suspenseful without giving away the surprise ending.

Now is your chance to be a mystery writer! All good writers know it pays to plan before writing. Think about how the author used each element in *Surprise Island* and then decide what to include in your story. Use the questions below to guide you. Write brief notes on the lines provided. When you have planned the story elements, use the back of this paper to write your mystery. Include as many details as you can.

Plot

- What is the mystery in the book *Surprise Island?*

  _____

- What will be the mystery in your story?

  _____

- What clues did the author give to help the character, and the reader solve the mystery?

  _____

- What clues and events will lead to the solving of your mystery?

  _____

Setting

- Often, mystery stories are set in an unusual or exotic place or in a historical period. This adds to the mystery and suspense of the story. Think about how the setting of the island and the children being alone there add to the mystery of *Surprise Island*. When and where will your story take place?

  _____

- How will you use the setting as a part of the mystery?

  _____

Characters

- Who will the characters be in your story?

  _____

- Mysteries usually include lots of suspense and action. Sometimes they have some scary episodes that make the reader want to keep reading to find out what will happen next. What parts of *Surprise Island* made you want to keep reading to find out what happens?

  _____

Time Capsule

An archaeological dig provides an opportunity to see what life was like in the distant past. The artifacts can help modern people understand the beliefs and values of older civilizations.

Work as a class or in small groups to complete the following activities.

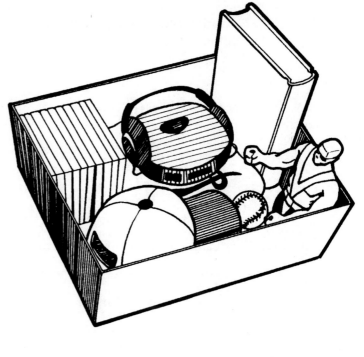

1. Many of the things found in dig sites are "garbage," or what is left behind. Make a list of things that would be considered garbage today. Not all the items on the list would last a long time. Sun and rain can cause certain materials to biodegrade over time. Draw a line through those items that would decay. What would be left for future archaeologists to find?

_____

_____

_____

_____

2. Brainstorm a list of things that represent you and your life. Include items from school and home. What things do you value most? Are they biodegradable? Which of these things might last for 1,000 years? Which probably will not last?

_____

_____

_____

_____

3. In some cultures structures—like the pyramids in Egypt—preserved things from everyday life. Today many buildings and events are marked with time capsules, special containers intended to preserve items of interest for future generations. Select items from the lists above and create a collection. Include the items you have value and things from your garbage. Arrange the items in a display as though you were a future archaeologist. Think about whether the use of each item would be clear to you.

Meet the Aldens

The Alden children work together and share many interests, like swimming, boating, and exploring. Each one also has different talents, skills, and interests. They use their skills to benefit each other and to solve mysteries. Add one more fact that you have learned from your reading to each of the descriptions below.

• Benny, the youngest Alden, is six years old. He makes friends very easily and knows how to catch the fish.

_____

• Violet likes to sew and takes her workbag with her to the island. She is learning to play the violin.

_____

• Jessie is very good at running the household. She organizes things and cooks many of the meals.

_____

• Henry, age 15, is the oldest of the Boxcar Children. He is good at building things.

_____

• Make an inventory list of your skills, talents, and interests.

_____

Choose one of the Alden children and complete the Venn diagram below to compare and contrast yourself to him or her.

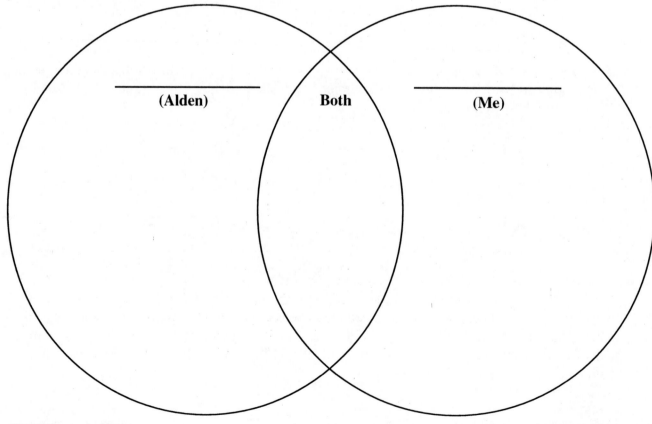

(Alden)   **Both**   (Me)

Any Questions?

Now that you have met the Aldens and read about their summer adventure, you may have some unanswered questions. On the back of this page, write any questions you may have about the summer's events or the future of the Boxcar Children.

Work in groups to prepare possible answers to questions that you and your classmates came up with and those on this page. When you have finished making your predictions, share your ideas with the class.

- What does Joe find when the shell pile is excavated?

- Do you think Violet will continue to play the violin?

- Grandfather wants to take a trip before school begins. Tell where you think they will go and what will happen.

- Does Henry grow up to work in a museum like Joe?

- Grandfather started a museum and donated money to build it. If you had a lot of money, what would you like to build for other people to enjoy?

- Jessie knew how to make an apple pie. Think of something you know how to do. Write directions so that someone else could follow them. Put them in proper order and be sure not to leave anything out.

- Do Pat and Johnny learn about water safety? Make a list of safety rules for boating and swimming.

- You are in charge of Benny's birthday party. Plan whom you will invite, what you will serve, and what games you will play.

- The children return to the island in the fall and explore the yellow house. Describe what they find there.

- What does Mike do with the money he found in the treasure chest?

- The note in the bottle was signed "J. A. and R. W." J. A. stands for James Alden, the children's grandfather. Who is R. W.?

Research Ideas

Are there things that you read about in *Surprise Island* that you would like to learn more about?
Work in groups to research and explore one of the topics from the list below or one that interested you as you read. Share your findings in an oral or written report, a poster, a science fair project, or another appropriate form.

clams	swimming	caves	violins
shells	fishing	islands	birds
tides	carpentry	gardening	flowers
seaweed	archaeology	sewing	Native American culture
boating	butterflies	cooking	John James Audubon
lobstering	flower drying		

Book Report Ideas

There are many ways to report on a book. After you have finished reading *Surprise Island* or another *Boxcar Children* story, choose a method of reporting that interests you. It may be a teacher's suggestion, an idea of your own, or one of the ways mentioned below.

❏ Pen Pal

Write a letter to one of the characters in your story. Tell him or her how similar and different your life is to his or hers. Ask questions of that character and offer your opinions about some of the situations in the story. Pretend that you are the character and write a letter back to yourself.

❏ The Funny Papers

Make a comic strip about one of the scenes in your story. Include a title frame and lots of conversation bubbles to retell what happened.

❏ TV Commercial

Write a TV commercial for the book and present it live to the class or produce a commercial on videotape and bring it in for viewing.

❏ Mobile Magic

Create and assemble a colorful mobile to display in your classroom. Using a coat hanger, string or fishing wire, and heavy paper, show the plot, setting, and characters of your story. Start by placing the setting at the top level, the characters at the middle level, and developing the plot at the bottom level.

❏ Patchwork Quilt

Use a piece of 18" x 26" (46 cm x 66 cm) tagboard and six 8" x 8" (20 cm x 20 cm) squares of paper. Glue the squares on the tagboard and simulate "stitching" around each piece using a crayon or marker. Each of the squares will tell specific information about your story. One square should state the title and author, and the other squares should tell about the characters, plot, and settings.

❏ Act It Out!

This report lends itself to a group project. A size-appropriate group prepares a scene from the story for dramatization, acts it out, and relates the significance of the scene to the entire book. Costumes and props will add to the dramatization.

❏ Dress and Guess!

Come to class dressed as one of the characters. Tell the class your version of the story from that character's perspective. Act like that character and answer any questions the class may have about you and your life.

❏ Literary Interview

This report is done in pairs. One student will pretend to be a character in the story, steeped completely in the persona of his or her character. The other student will play the role of a television or radio interviewer, trying to provide the audience with insights into the character's personality and life. It is the responsibility of the partners to create meaningful questions and appropriate responses.

Can You Guess?

Step 1: Select a character from your story or book.

Step 2: Fill in the following sentence clues about your chosen character.

Clue #1: If I were to tell you how my character looks, I would say that . . .

_____

_____

_____

Clue #2: Something my character said was . . .

_____

_____

_____

Clue #3: Something my character did was...

_____

_____

_____

Clue #4: I think the story could/could not (circle one) have happened without my character because . . .

_____

_____

_____

Step 3: Read one clue at a time to the class. At the end of each clue, see if anyone can identify your character. If no one can guess correctly after the last clue, you may tell the class the name of your character and show a drawing of your character.

Sequence of Events

Note to the Teacher: Write a series of events from the story in jumbled sequence and then have the students cut them apart and paste them in the correct order on construction paper.

_____

Name of Book or Story

Q and A

This is a stimulating, cooperative-learning game that employs all levels of Bloom's Taxonomy skills. The dynamics of the game are such that all students can participate successfully and are engaged at all times. Play "Q and A" before administering tests, or use this activity as an assessment form itself. There are a number of ways to play the game, and as you run through "Q and A" a few times you will probably want to customize the game to best suit your needs and the needs of your students.

Materials

- standard-size tagboard
- 25 self-adhesive pockets (the kind used in library books for checkout cards)
- 25 colored, circle stickers—5 each of 5 different colors
- 25 index cards (to fit into library pockets)
- 6 rulers or 1' (31 cm) sticks like paint stirrers
- 6 different colored oval shapes with 10" (25 cm) diameters
- colored marker

Set-up of Game Board

1. Place the pockets on the tagboard to form five rows of five and then stick the backs to the tagboard.
2. Determine which color each row will be.
3. Starting with the first row (horizontally), place one color of sticker circles on the upper, front part of the pocket card. Continue placing stickers on all five pockets in that row.
4. Determine the colors for the next rows, and repeat the process until the entire board represents five different-colored rows of pockets with sticker circles.
5. Starting with the top row again, use a marker to write a large number "10" on each of the cards in the first column.
6. Use the same procedure for the next four columns, writing "20," "30," "40," and "50."

Game Board Suggestions

Laminate the board with the pockets glued on for durability. Have an adult use a razor blade to cut open each pocket.

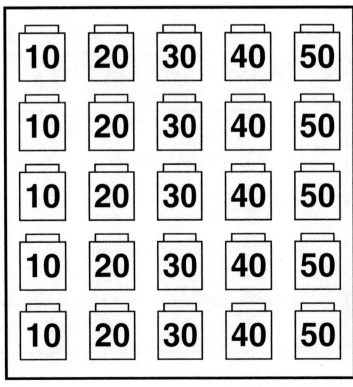

Q and A *(cont.)*

How to Play

- Arrange the students into six groups of five or whatever works for your class.

- Place a game stick at each table.

- On the board, write down the six different colors for each group for score-keeping purposes.

- Begin with one group and rotate in a clockwise fashion.

- Each team member will have an opportunity to hold the game stick. Even though team members collaborate on the answers and decisions that need to be made, only the person holding the game stick is allowed to speak for the group. The game stick is rotated clockwise after each team's turn.

- The game-show host or hostess will ask that team to decide which color card and point value they wish to try. The host then reads the card aloud for the whole class to hear. Give the team about one minute to discuss possible answers. While this team is thinking, the other teams should also be doing the same since they may have an opportunity to answer this question at a later time.

- The game-stick holder will then answer the question. If the answer is correct, that team receives the points marked on that pocket, and the game stick then moves on to the next team. If the team does not answer the question correctly, the next team in the rotation has a chance to steal the points.

- If the next team answers the previous question correctly, they get the points for that card and then may also choose another card to answer. If the second team cannot answer the "steal" question, then the card simply goes back into its place, and they still get to choose a question.

- This procedure continues throughout the course of the game until all the cards have been answered.

- The object of "Q and A" is to be the team with the most points at the end of the game. Teams take turns answering the questions, with each member of each team also having a turn to speak. The game is finished when all the cards have been answered correctly.

Rules and Guidelines

✓ Only the person holding the game stick may speak for the group.

✓ All responses to questions must be discussed with the entire group before answering. If the game-stick holder speaks before collaboration, then the team loses its turn.

✓ The majority of the team must agree on the response before it is presented to the host or hostess.

✓ Teams may respond only when it is their turn.

Q and A *(cont.)*

Setup of Game Sticks

1. Write "Q and A" in large print on each of the colored oval shapes.

2. Laminate the shapes for durability.

3. Tape or glue each shape to a stick or ruler to make a sign. (See illustration.)

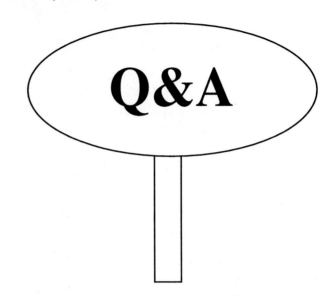

Setup of Game Cards

1. The questions for "Q and A" range from easy to challenging. All 10-point questions are at the Bloom's knowledge level, beginning with "who," "when," or "what." The 50-point questions will adhere to the Synthesis and Evaluation levels, asking students to modify, judge, classify, and evaluate. (A suggested questioning chart according to Bloom's Taxonomy is included on page 42.)

2. With the card held lengthwise, write the point value in the center of the card. On the back of the card, write the question at the top and the answer at the bottom.

3. Place the cards in their appropriate pocket slot with the point value showing.

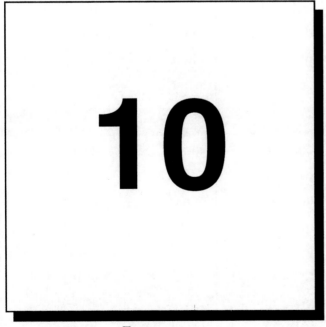

10

Front

Q: What is Joe's real name?

A: John Joseph Alden

Back

Q and A (cont.)

Helpful Hints

- The questions may be created by the teacher or by students.

- You may want to provide the option of "bonus" cards. Behind one or two cards, place a "bonus" card that provides another question and opportunity for points.

- Play the game in a *Jeopardy!* style where the host reads the answer, and the students must come up with the possible question.

- To promote good listening skills, the host or hostess should read the question only two times. This encourages the students to repeat the question to each other.

- If you will be offering prizes for the winners, be sure to offer a prize to the teams who worked well cooperatively. Competition is fun and necessary but use every opportunity to affirm successful teamwork.

Bloom's Verbs

Knowledge		Comprehension		Application	
label	name	tell	explain	transfer	use
sequence	recall	generalize	paraphrase	apply	select
describe	list	discuss	summarize	compute	demonstrate
quote	draw	locate	review	show	prepare
recite	define	identify	interpret	produce	interview
write	count	illustrate	demonstrate	change	dramatize
tell	match	report	predict	choose	draw
find	identify	restate	conclude	paint	imitate

Analysis		Synthesis		Evaluation	
differentiate	debate	create	construct	judge	appraise
compare	analyze	produce	originate	predict	conclude
contrast	research	design	develop	select	rank
outline	discriminate	compose	integrate	rate	assess
deduce	distinguish	propose	plan	prove	criticize
characterize	examine	invent	rewrite	choose	justify
classify	relate	organize	make up	decide	prioritize
separate	diagram	pretend	perform	evaluate	argue

A Grand Opening

Hold a grand opening party to show off the new museum. Assign small groups or work as a class to plan the celebration.

Guest List

- Decide who will be invited to the opening—parents, school officials, other classes, etc. Create invitations using card stock and dried flowers, a seashell, or a design suggested by the children.

- Send or deliver the invitations at least a week in advance.

Program

- Complete all displays. Assign a group of students to each area of the museum. They will act as curators to make sure the displays are complete.

- Assign students to serve as hosts for the event. Station them near the door to greet visitors and distribute museum brochures to the guests as they arrive.

- Appoint several students to act as tour guides. Have them write a script that gives a brief synopsis of the book and explains the various projects and exhibits.

- Have some students demonstrate the method used to dry flowers.

- Set up a "Sandbox Archaeology" display and ask guests to participate.

- Conduct a session of "Q and A."

- If desired, small groups may select a favorite scene from the book to re-enact for the guests.

Refreshments

Plan to serve simple foods, drawing on items mentioned in the book or ask the students to contribute samples of their recipes from the "Island Cookbook."

Objective Test

Matching: Match each word with its correct meaning.

1. _____ practice
2. _____ clever
3. _____ handy
4. _____ collection
5. _____ interesting
6. _____ dozen
7. _____ trouble
8. _____ lesson

a. twelve of something
b. to do something over and over, to become skilled at it
c. skillful, smart
d. something to be learned
e. easily reached or used

f. things that have been collected or gathered
g. exciting or of interest to someone
h. problems or worries

True or False: Write *true* or *false* next to each statement below.

1. _____ The Alden children are afraid to take care of themselves.
2. _____ Grandfather sends the children to the island because he does not like them.
3. _____ Benny thinks his teddy bear is the most important thing to bring along to the island.
4. _____ The children can get supplies each day when Joe goes to the mainland in the boat.
5. _____ No one had lived on the island before the Aldens.
6. _____ Joe asks the children to keep the shell pile a secret.
7. _____ While they are on the island, Violet learns to play the piano.
8. _____ The children are happy to learn that Joe is their cousin.

Short Answer: Write a short answer for each of these questions.

1. How do the children find out more about the nature items they found on the island?

   _____

   _____

2. Who lived on the island long ago?

   _____

   _____

3. Where does Grandfather take the children?

   _____

   _____

4. Who does not want to be seen by Grandfather?

   _____

   _____

5. Who has a birthday while they are on the island?

   _____

   _____

Essay: Answer these questions on the back of this paper.

1. Do you think that Watch is a good dog? Describe why.
2. Describe at least two surprises that happened on the island.

3. Explain why Joe was a strange handyman.
4. Write about lobsters and lobster fishing.

Conversations

Cut the converstion strips and distribute one to each group of students. Have groups write and perform the conversations that might have occurred in each situation.

Before the book begins, Henry, Jessie, Violet, and Benny try to guess what surprise Grandfather has planned for them. (4 people)

Mr. Alden's father arranges to buy the island from its previous owner.
(2 people)

Joe goes back to thank the old Indian for helping him to get well. (2 people)

Joe explains to Henry and Jessie how to take care of their garden.
(3 people)

Henry, Jessie, and Violet comfort Benny when he becomes homesick.
(4 people)

Grandfather tells the children stories of his adventures on the island when he was a boy. (Grandfather + any number of children)

Benny tells Joe and Captain Daniel about the trip to the museum. (3 people)

Henry explains to Mr. Browning that they can not invite him in because he is a stranger. (2 people)

Johnny and Pat apologize to the person whose boat they took. (3 people)

Benny tells his teddy bear about all of his best friends and why he likes them. (1 person and 1 teddy bear)

Grandfather discusses with Dr. Moore the next adventure he has planned for the children. (2 people)

Bibliography of Related Reading

Fiction

Bradbury, Bianca. *Two on an Island*. Houghton Mifflin Company, 1976.

Cole, Joanna. *The Magic School Bus on the Ocean Floor*. Scholastic, 1994.

Cummings, Priscilla. *Chadwick and the Garplegrungen*. Tidewater Publishers, 1987.

Holling, Holling C. *Seabird*. Houghton Mifflin Company, 1978.

O'Dell, Scott. *Island of the Blue Dolphins*. Dell Publishing Company, 1987.

Taylor, Theodore. *The Cay*. Camelot, 1995.

Warner, Gertrude Chandler. *Surprise Island*. Albert Whitman and Company, 1977.

> *Bicycle Mystery*. Albert Whitman and Company, 1990.
> *Blue Bay Mystery*. Albert Whitman and Company, 1990.
> *Caboose Mystery*. Albert Whitman and Company, 1990.
> *Mountaintop Mystery*. Albert Whitman and Company, 1990.
> *Schoolhouse Mystery*. Albert Whitman and Company, 1989.
> *The Yellow House Mystery*. Albert Whitman and Company, 1989.

Nonfiction References

Aspinwall, Karen. *The Down by the Sea Activity Book*. The Cattail Company, 1993.

Ballantine, Todd. *Tideland Treasure*. University of South Carolina Press, 1991.

Behm, Barbara J. and Veronica Bonar. *Exploring Seashores*. Gareth Stevens Publishing, 1994.

Blain, Diane. *The Boxcar Children Cookbook*. Albert Whitman and Company, 1991.

Carpenter, Mimi Gregoire. *What the Sea Left Behind*. Down East Books, 1981.

Center for Marine Conservation. *The Ocean Book*. John Wiley and Sons, 1989.

Coldrey, Jennifer and Deni Bown. *Eyewitness Explorers: Shells*. Dorling Kindersley, Inc., 1998.

Coulombe, Deborah (in cooperation with the University of New Hampshire). *The Seaside Naturalist*. Simon and Shuster, 1992.

Ellsworth, Mary Ellen. *Gertrude Chandler Warner and the Boxcar Children*. Albert Whitman and Company, 1997.

Griggs, Jack L. *All the Birds of North America: American Bird Conservancy's Field Guide*. HarperCollins, 1997.

Harrison, George H. and Kit Harrison. *Backyard Bird Watching for Kids: How to Attract, Feed, and Provide Homes for Birds*. Willow Creek, 1997.

Hood, Susan. *Wildflowers (National Audubon Society First Field Guide)*. Scholastic, 1998.

Ricciuti, Edward R. *Rocks and Minerals (National Audubon Society First Field Guides)*. Scholastic, 1998.

Answer Key

Page 10

1. Accept appropriate answers.
2. The children's surprise is spending the summer on the island.
3. Accept reasonable answers.
4. Some possible answers include dishes, pail, clothes, shoes, food, tools, flashlight, and a teddy bear.
5. Benny thought that his teddy bear was the most important thing.
6. Accept reasonable answers.
7. They leave their list in the box on the dock and Captain Daniel or Joe brings what the children need from the mainland.
8. Benny's job is to take the order to the box each day and to get the groceries and mail when they arrive.
9. Accept reasonable answers.
10. Accept reasonable answers.

Page 13

1. $4 \times 3 = 12$
2. $4 \times 2 = 8$
3. $3 \times 2 = 6$
4. $5 \times 3 = 15$
5. $6 \times 4 = 24$
6. $2 \times 6 = 12$
7. $4 \times 5 = 20$
8. $2 \times 7 = 14$
9. $3 \times 6 = 18$
10. $2 \times 7 = 14$

Page 15

1. Accept appropriate answers.
2. He saw them shooting water from beneath the sand.
3. Watch helps dig up the clams.
4. Benny said the water was too cold. Joe convinced Benny to get in the water to see the seaweed.
5. He knew the names of all kinds of seaweed.

6. Henry suggests that they make a museum. The other children agree.
7. Accept reasonable answers.
8. Benny knew that Joe got two newspapers every day.
9. The roof leaked.
10. Accept reasonable answers.

Page 18

Answers will vary.

Page 20

1. Accept reasonable answers.
2. Indians had lived in the cave.
3. The tide came in while the children were in it.
4. Accept reasonable answers.
5. Because of the arrowhead, ax head, and shell pile the children found, Joe knew that Indians had lived in the area.
6. Including people in the photo would help to show the size of the shell pile.
7. Indians did not have horses before the Europeans came.
8. If others learned of the site, they might come and disturb the area before it could be properly examined.
9. Henry names it Indian Point
10. She thought it would be selfish to practice violin rather than help the others work.

Page 25

1. Accept appropriate answers.
2. Accept reasonable answers.
3. It was hot up there.
4. Grandfather shows them his museum, especially the room devoted to his first collection of birds, made when he was 15.
5. Accept reasonable answers.

Answer Key *(cont.)*

6. Mr. Browning came looking for a lost friend and was invited to share the children's dinner.

7. The children told Mr. Browning that Joe knew about flowers, birds, clams, shells, and Indian things.

8. Mike continues digging and finds the buried treasure.

9. They steal it.

10. Accept reasonable answers.

Page 30

1. Accept reasonable answers.

2. Benny wanted a little bottle of cream so that he could have blackberries with cream like Peter Rabbit.

3. They liked the idea of Joe living with them.

4. Accept reasonable answers.

5. It was his birthday.

6. The children feared that a sudden surprise might cause grandfather to go into shock.

7. Alden Island was renamed Surprise Island because of for all the surprises found there.

8. Captain Daniel told Dr. Moore about Joe and introduced them on the day the children moved to the island.

9. All of the artifacts will be placed on display in a museum.

10. Grandfather is the children's best friend.

Page 44

Matching

1. b
2. c
3. e
4. f
5. g
6. a
7. h
8. d

True or False

1. False
2. False
3. True
4. True
5. False
6. True
7. False
8. True

Short Answer

1. library books
2. Indians
3. Museum
4. Joe
5. Benny

Essay

Accept reasonable answers.

Page 45

Perform the conversations in class. Ask students to respond to the presentations in various ways, such as, "Are the conversations realistic?" or "Are the words the characters are saying appropriate for their characters?"